THE NUTTY INTERNET JOKE BOOK

belongs to

_____

The NUTTY INTERNET Joke Book

JOHN BYRNE

RED FOX

For Sheila
www.sheilaferguson.com

A Red Fox Book

Published by Random House Children's Books
20 Vauxhall Bridge Road, London SW1V 2SA

A division of The Random House Group Ltd
London Melbourne Sydney Auckland
Johannesburg and agencies throughout the world

Text and illustrations copyright © John Byrne 2001

1 3 5 7 9 10 8 6 4 2

Typeset by SX Composing DTP, Rayleigh, Essex
Printed and bound in Great Britain by
Cox & Wyman Limited, Reading, Berkshire

THE RANDOM HOUSE GROUP Limited Reg No. 954009

www.randomhouse.co.uk

ISBN 0 09 940905 4

INTER-DUCTION

HELLO FELLOW NET NUTS!

Welcome to a worldwidewebful of complete Net nuttiness! Whether you're already nuts about the Net or the only computer you use is counting on your fingers, you can count on me to keep you laughing until log off time.

So what are you waiting for? Get surfing!

I'll P.C. you later!

Where is Pinocchio's website?
On the splinternet.

What do you get if you type
www.abcdefghijklmnopqrstuvwxyz.com
into your computer?
A sore finger.

What do you get if you cross a constable
with a computer?
P.C. Plod.

WHAT DID YOU SAY TO THE POLICEMAN WHO SPENT EIGHT HOURS ON THE INTERNET?

"OH GIVE IT ARREST..."

"I think I'm spending too long on the
Internet, I'm starting to get spots in front
of my eyes.
  "Have you seen an optician?"
  "No, just spots."

Why did the skunk redesign his website?
Because everyone said it stank.

What do you call someone who spends 24
  hours a day on the Internet?
*Anything you like, they're not listening to
  you anyway.*

HAVE YOU SEEN THE ALARM CLOCK WEBSITE?

YES BUT I DIDN'T THINK IT WAS VERY STRIKING...

Where do you find smelly Internet sites?
On your hum computer.

"Have you got the address of the butter
  website?"
  "Yes, but don't spread it around."

INTERNUTTY KNOW-HOW 1

SURF SAFELY!

The Internet has a whole world of exciting things to explore, but like any other world it can have its nasty side, too. Here are some tips to make sure that your surfing is as safe and fun as possible. You'd be nuts to ignore them!

1. Never give out any personal information, like your last name, phone number and address, or the name and address of your school, over the Net without your parents' or a teacher's permission. This also goes for sending things via ordinary post to addresses you see on the Net.

2. Be careful about giving out your e-mail address . . . at the very least you could end up with lots and lots of unwanted junk mail.

3. Be careful of any special offers or "something for nothing" deals you see advertised on the Net. Don't send money for anything without checking with your parents first . . . and don't ever give their credit card details over the Net.

4. Always remember to "log out" when you finish surfing. You don't want to accidentally leave the computer connected and run up a big phone bill.

5. If you receive any messages or see anything that makes you uncomfortable while using the Net, tell your parents or a teacher immediately, just as you would if someone was bothering you in real life.

6. Remember that the Internet is like any other activity – it is even more interesting and fun when you take a break every now and again to enjoy other hobbies and exercises.

Why did the internut bury his laptop?
The batteries were dead.

"So what exactly can I learn on the Internet?"

"Anything you like – it can even teach you to talk like an Indian."

"How?"

"See? It's working already!"

TEACHER: If you spend all your time sitting round playing on the Internet, you'll be fat and useless when you grow up.

PUPIL: Wow! You must have spent *hours* surfing when you were a kid!

WHY DID YOU
BRING YOUR HOME
COMPUTER INTO
THE CLASSROOM?

I WANTED
AN APPLE
FOR THE
TEACHER.

"Do you want some help using the Internet, son?"

"No thanks, Dad, I can muck it up all by myself."

WHAT KIND OF MACHINE COUNTS SHEEP?

A HOME COMP-EWE-TER!

INTERNUT: Sorry I'm late for school. I dreamt I was surfing the web.

TEACHER: How could that make you late for school?

INTERNUT: I had to go back to sleep to switch off the computer.

FIRST INTERNUT: The CD rom keeps falling out of my computer. What can I use to keep it in?

SECOND INTERNUT: How about a paper bag?

FIRST INTERNUT: I'm a bit worried about letting you repair my expensive computer.

SECOND INTERNUT: Don't worry, in all my years of repairing computers, only one has ever blown up.

FIRST INTERNUT: How many computers have you repaired, then?

SECOND INTERNUT: This will be my second.

"Doctor, doctor, my little brother thinks he's a computer."

"Well bring him in so I can cure him."

"I can't, I need to use him to finish my homework."

The internut took his seat at the school
computer.
But the teacher made him put it back.

Why did the internut bite the school
computer?
Someone told him it was an Apple.

Who was using his laptop when he fell
off the wall?
Humpt e-Dumpty.

Why did the internut stick bread in his
disk drive?
Someone told him to use his loaf.

"Doctor, doctor, I've spent so long at my P.C. that I've got double vision."

"Well, go around with one eye shut."

WAK-E, WAK-E!

WHAT DO YOU SAY TO AN INTERNUT FIRST THING IN THE MORNING?

What do internuts eat for breakfast?
Mice Clickspies.

"Do you turn on your computer with your left hand or your right hand?"

"My right hand."

"Amazing! Most people have to use the on/off switch."

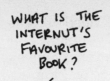

WHAT IS THE INTERNUT'S FAVOURITE BOOK?

"THE ONLINE, THE SWITCH AND THE WWW.ARDROBE"!

"Have you seen
www.custardjellyandicecream.com?"
"Yes, it's a trifle boring."

"Have you seen the hypnosis website?"
"Yes, but it put me to sleep."

WHAT DID THE HYPNOTIST SAY WHEN HE GOT HIS OWN WEBSITE...

HYP, HYP, HOORAY

FIRST INTERNUT: There's a hole in the
school computer screen.
SECOND INTERNUT: Don't worry, the
science teacher is looking into it.

"Have you seen *www.dustbin.com*?"
"Yes, but it's a load of rubbish."

WHY COULDN'T THE ALLIGATOR SEND E-MAILS ON HIS PC?

BECAUSE IT WAS AN OLD CROC.

"This computer you charged me £950 for
doesn't work . . . and you said it would be
trouble free."

"It is. I charged you £950 for the
computer, but you're getting all that
trouble absolutely free!"

What is an internut's favourite food?
Fish and microchips.

DO YOU ENJOY WEBSURFING?

NO WAY! MY MUM WARNED WE TO STAY AWAY FROM THE NET!

Why did the internut set fire to his
  computer?
He wanted to have the hottest website.

"Have you heard about
www.opticians.com?"
"Yes, it's a site for sore eyes."

What did one mouse say to the other
  mouse?
I get a click out of you.

WHAT DID THE MOUSE SAY TO THE WEBCAM?

CHEESE.

17

"Have you seen *www.skeletons.com*?"
"Yes, it's a rattling good website."

"Have you seen *www.verylowwall.com*?"
"No, I must have overlooked it."

"Well, have you seen
www.veryhighwall.com?"
"Yes, I couldn't get over it."

"Have you seen the dynamite website?"
"Yes, it really blew my mind."

Why didn't the internut get any e-mail?
*Because his e-dog kept chasing the
e-postman.*

What do you get if you cross Star Wars
   with the Internet?
e-threepio.

WHAT DID DARTH VADER
SAY TO THE INTERNET?

"MAY THE
FORCE
E-WITH
YOU..."

Knock, knock.
Who's there?
Saturn.
Saturn Who?
*Saturn front of the computer all day
and still couldn't work out how to use
the Net.*

WHAT DID
THE SAUSAGE
SAY WHEN IT
COULDN'T
LOG ON
TO THE
INTERNET?

"IF AT FIRST
YOU DON'T
SUCCEED
FRY, FRY
AGAIN..."

"Have you seen *www.tomatosauce.com?*"
"No, I'll ketchup with it later,"

"Have you seen *www.hook.com?*"
"Yes, it's already caught my eye."

"Have you seen *www.amnesia.com?*"
"Sorry, I just can't remember."

"Have you seen *www.usedmatch.com?*"
"Yes, but I didn't find it striking."

What do robots put at the bottom of
their e-mails?
Yours tin-sincerely.

What do werewolves put at the bottom of
their e-mails?
Beast wishes.

"Have you seen
www.shelterfromtherain.com?"
"Yes, but it doesn't really stand out."

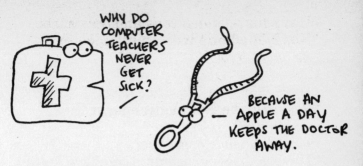

WHY DO COMPUTER TEACHERS NEVER GET SICK?

BECAUSE AN APPLE A DAY KEEPS THE DOCTOR AWAY.

"What's the difference between your finger and a hammer?"

"I don't know."

"Well, you're not using my computer keyboard then!"

Who sits at the end of the yellow brick
road surfing the Net?
The www.izard of Oz.

WHAT DOES DOROTHY WEAR WHEN SHE SURFS THE NET?

HER RUB—E. SLIPPERS

21

What's hairy, dangerous and only surfs
the Net when there's a full moon?
The www.erewolf.

Who surfs the Net by pecking at the
keyboard?
www.oody www.oodpecker.

Who runs the 100 acre wood website?
www.innie the pooh.

WHAT'S THE
BEST PLACE IN
THE WOODS
TO WEBSURF?

THE
TED E-BEARS
PICNIC

"How are you getting on with the
Internet?"
"Surf far, so good."

How did the internut feel when he first
started websurfing?
It was love at first site.

How does the vicar explore the Internet?
With the church mouse.

What do internuts drink at breaktime?
Netscafe.

"Doctor, doctor, I don't think I'm a
computer anymore. Now I think I'm
a desk."

"You're just letting things get on
top of you."

"My computer isn't electric, it's clockwork."

"Really?"

"No, I was just winding you up."

*

"Doctor, doctor, my computer screen is giving me a headache."

"Why's that?"

"I keep banging my head on it."

What is an internut's favourite Italian food?

Mac-aroni.

HOW DO ITALIAN CHEFS SWAP RECIPES?

BY SPAGHETT-E MAIL!

"You're spending a lot of time at that computer screen. Have you had your eyes checked?"

"No, they've always been blue."

How do you stop your laptop batteries
    from running out?
Hide their trainers.

"Which kind of ink do you put in your
computer's printer? Black, Red or Iced?"
    "Iced ink?"
    "Well, yes you do, but I didn't want to
mention it."

Where do web surfers dance?
At a netball.

Where does an elephant carry its laptop?
In its trunk.

What do wimpy internuts programme into
   their computers?
Softyware

"Mum, Mum, Dad's broken my
computer!"
   "How did he do that?"
   "I dropped it on his head."

"Have you seen *www.northpole.com*?"
"Yes, but it left me cold."

"Have you seen *www.topsecret.com*?"
"If I have, I'm not going to tell you."

How do vampire bats surf the Internet?
With their flaptop computers.

How do ghosts avoid eye strain when they
use the Internet?
They always wear spooktacles.

"Why do you keep going back to that
fishing website?"
   "I can't help it, I'm hooked."

How do whales type e-mails?
With their fish fingers.

INTERNUTTY KNOW-HOW 2

NOW YOU'RE TALKING...

Even before the Internet existed (back in the dark ages), having pen pals was a great way of chatting to people all over the world and getting the lowdown on what was cool in other countries. Now you can have pen pals on the Internet, only they are called "key pals". You don't have to wait so long for letters and messages to arrive and with plenty of "chat rooms" on the Net you can speak to lots of key pals at once and share gossip from all over the world.

HOW DO YOU FIND THE COOLEST E-PALS OF ALL?

CHOOSE ONES WHO LIVE IN SIBERIA!

Here are some cool sites that will allow you to find key pals and exchange messages safely.

http//:www.headbone.com

http//:chat.freezone.com

http//:www.mightymedia.com/keypals/

Why couldn't the baby camel surf the
  Internet?
*Because whenever his parents saw their
  phone bill they got the hump.*

"Helpline? I've just pushed a piece of
bacon into my disk drive."
  "Has the computer stopped working?"
  "No, but there's lots of crackling."

What do you get if you stuff your
  computer's disk drive with herbs?
A thyme machine.

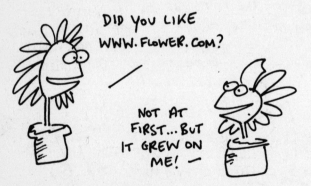

What do you get if you cross
  a computer with a hamburger?
A Big Mac.

"Doctor, doctor, I'm so big I can't fit at my computer terminal."

"Have you tried to diet?"

"Yes, but no matter what colour it is, I still can't fit."

Where does the Internet football team play?
Webley.

How do Leprechauns get on the Internet?
They use their gnome computers.

How do ghosts type e-mails?
They use a skeleton keyboard.

Where's Spiderman's home page?
On the world wide web.

Why did the duck stick his leg into
a computer?
He wanted to have webbed feet.

What do computer experts do at
weekends?
Go for a disk drive.

WHY DID THE
CHICKEN CROSS
THE WEB?

TO GET
TO THE
OTHER
SITE!

Why did Granny stick her head in a disk
drive?
*Someone told her she should put her hair
in a Net.*

Where do snowmen put their webpages?
On the winternet.

What did the parrot say when he was
   using the Internet?
"P.C.s of eight, P.C.s of eight."

WHAT DO
YOU SAY TO
AN
INTERNET
PARROT?

"WHO'S A
PRETT-E
BOY
THEN?"

How did the princess find out
   Rumplestiltskin's name?
She looked on his gnome page.

What do you get if you take your
   computer to an ice rink?
A slipped disk.

Why did the farmer hang raincoats all
   over his orchard?
*Someone told him he should get an apple
   mac.*

How do internuts dance?
Slow, slow, click, click, slow.

Who is the oldest singer on the Internet?
Click Jagger.

Why do beavers spend a fortune on the
  Internet?
They never want to log off.

WHAT'S FURRY AND ALWAYS ON THE INTERNET?

AN E-GER BEAVER!

What do you get if you cross an elephant
  and a P.C.?
A computer with a really big memory.

Why did the school bully kick the
  classroom computer?
*Someone told him he was supposed to boot
  up the system.*

Why do goalkeepers spend ages on the
   Internet?
Because they can't stop saving their work.

Why did the internut paint his computer
   screen in little black and white squares?
He wanted to check his e-mail.

"Have you seen
www.needleinahaystack.com?"
"Yes, but it took ages to find."

"Have you seen
www.lipstickpowderandpaint.com?"
"Oh come on, you just made that one up!"

"Have you seen *www.apathy.com*?"
"No, and quite honestly I can't be
   bothered."

Where do you find internut snails?
At the end of an internut's fingers.

Why are elephants no good at Net
   surfing?
Because they're scared of the mouse.

Why didn't the boy mouse get on with
   the girl mouse?
They just didn't click.

Have you seen the new fishing website?
No, it's not online yet.

What surfs the Internet and goes, "Choo, Choo"?
Thomas the Search Engine.

Who has the best website in the jungle?
The Onlion King.

What happened when the school bully
  went netsurfing?
*The goalkeeper kicked him out of the
  football ground.*

"Have you seen *www.indecisive.com*?"
"Yes and no."

"I bought this computer yesterday and I
found a twig in the disk drive."
  "I'm sorry, sir, you'll have to speak to
the branch manager."

Why was the hen banned from sending
  e-mails?
She was always using fowl language.

What does the invisible man say when he's on the Internet?
"Now you e me, now you don't."

∗

"Excuse me, this computer has a cake instead of a plug."
"Yes, sir, it's a currant bun."

Why did the internut put his computer in the fridge?
He wanted to find some really cool sites.

What's the best city to search the World
Wide Web in?
Rome.

@

Why couldn't the apple send an e-mail to
the orange?
Because the lime was engaged.

What's furry, curly and always eats
porridge before surfing the Net?
Goldilocks and the e-bears.

WHO'S BEEN SURFING ON OUR WEB?

I CAN'T BEAR TO TELL YOU...

Why did the dish and spoon hide their
computer?
The cat kept fiddling with i.t.

"Have you seen *www.quicksand.com*?"
"Yes, but it hasn't sunk in yet."

Who sits on Cinderella's keyboard? *Buttons.*

WHY WAS CINDERELLA ABLE TO SURF THE WEB?

BECAUSE HER FOOTMAN TURNED INTO A MOUSE.

GLASS

TEACHER: You've been e-mailing other pupils that I'm ugly!
PUPIL: Sorry, miss, I didn't realise you wanted to keep it a secret.

How do skunks send e-mail? *On their com-phew-ters.*

HOW DO SKUNKS LIKE THEIR E-MAILS?

SCENT.

What did the 98-year-old internut put in
his laptop?
Long life batteries.

How did the cow feel when they sent her
an e-mail?
She was over the moon.

"Have you seen *www.postalstrike.com*?"
"Yes, but it's nothing to write home
about."

WHY DON'T YOU STAMP E-MAILS?

BECAUSE YOUR FOOT WOULD GO RIGHT THROUGH THE COMPUTER SCREEN!

"What do you say to an internut on his
birthday?"
"For e's a jolly good fellow."

Why did the internut stick a chicken in
his computer?
Someone told him she was a battery hen.

What did the internut bring his keyboard
  to the disco?
He wanted to tap dance.

"Doctor, doctor, I keep thinking I'm a
laptop computer."
  "You're just run down, let me give you
some vitamins."
  "No, thanks. But I could do with some
new batteries."

Why did the computer act crazy?
It had a screw loose.

INTERNUTTY KNOW-HOW 3

HAVE YOU GOT THE WRITE STUFF?

The Net is full of cool sites and fascinating facts to read about and visit, but if you're a real internut you won't be happy just looking at other people's stuff; you'll want to take your own place in cyberspace. There are lots of programmes which will help you set up your own website, but you should also check out these websites and online magazines, which are written for kids by kids.

http//:www.kidscom.com

http//nces.ed.gov/nceskids/crunch/

http//www.zuzu.org/

In some cases you can enter your jokes, poems and short stories for competitions, or simply have them displayed on the web for other internuts to enjoy. At the very least you might be inspired to come up with a nutty Internet joke book all of your own!

WE'RE SUPPOSED TO DO AN· ARTICLE ABOUT DREAMS... BUT WE'VE BEEN UP ALL NIGHT THINKING WHAT TO WRITE

What did one keyboard say to the other
    keyboard?
Sorry, you're not my type.

What should you do if you get lots of
e-mails saying, "What's up, Doc? What's
up, Doc?"
Check for Bugs in your system.

What's green and scaly and surfs the
    web?
The Loch Net Monster.

Why did the internut put his laptop in
    the bath?
*He heard that the batteries had been
    drained.*

What did Hamlet say when he was
thinking of sending a message?
To e or not to e, that is the question.

"Want to buy a pocket computer?"
"No, thanks, I already know how many
pockets I've got."

How do nuns surf the web?
On the Hymnternet.

Why did the mummy stop using the
   Internet?
He was getting far too wrapped up in it.

How do musicians surf the web?
On the Violinternet.

How do wizards turn on their computers?
They press the on/off witch.

What did the giant say when he was
   surfing the web?
e-fi-fo-fum.

"Have you seen *www.quasimodo.com*?"
"I'm not sure, but it certainly rings a
   bell."

Where is the best place to buy computer software?
Washington C.D.

Which batteries do skunks use in their laptops?
Durasmells.

What do you get if you cross an elephant with a portable computer?
Very tired arms.

How does the joker surf the web?
On the Grinternet.

TEACHER: Why are you pushing garlic into the computer's disk drive?
PUPIL: To keep vampires off the Internet.
TEACHER: But there aren't any vampires on the Internet.
PUPIL: See? It works, doesn't it?

"I tried to send an e-mail and broke my computer."
"How do you manage that?"
"I think it was when I tried to push it through the letterbox."

CUSTOMER: I cleaned my computer and now it doesn't work any more.
REPAIRMAN: What did you clean it with?
CUSTOMER: Soap and water.
REPAIRMAN: Don't you know you're not supposed to touch a computer with water?
CUSTOMER: Oh, it wasn't the water that caused the problem . . . it was the spin dryer.

WHY DO YOU THINK YOUR REPORT SHOULD BE ON THE NET?

BECAUSE MY MARKS ARE ALL "E"s.

TEACHER: What are the four elements?
PUPIL: Fire, earth, water and the Internet.
TEACHER: What do you mean the Internet?
PUPIL: Well, Mum says that whenever I'm on the Net, I'm in my element.

51

PUPIL: Sir, would you mind e-mailing my exam results to my parents?

TEACHER: But your parents don't have a computer.

PUPIL: Exactly!

*

"I hope you're not one of those pupils who spends all day on the Net and doesn't get any exercise."

"Oh no, miss, I often sit around watching TV and not getting exercise either."

CUSTOMER: I think I've got a bug in my computer.

REPAIRMAN: Does your computer make a humming noise?

CUSTOMER: Yes.

REPAIRMAN: Then it must be a humbug.

WHAT DO YOU DO IF YOUR COMPUTER HUMS?

TELL IT TO CHANGE ITS SOCKS!

What did the maths homework website
   say to the geometry website?
Boy do we have problems.

Why did the internut keep a ruler by his
   computer?
To see how long he spent on the Net.

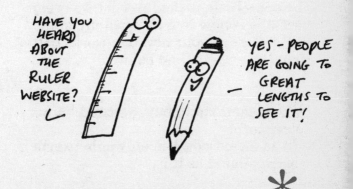

HAVE YOU HEARD ABOUT THE RULER WEBSITE?

YES - PEOPLE ARE GOING TO GREAT LENGTHS TO SEE IT!

Why do witches never get website
   addresses wrong?
Because they are very good at spelling.

"If you don't stop tapping away at that
keyboard I think I'll go crazy."
   "I think you already have, I stopped
using the keyboard an hour ago."

CAN YOU SHOW ME HOW TO USE THE NET?

I'D BETTER—OTHERWISE YOU'LL JUST GO ROUND AND ROUND IN CIRCLES.

"I never thought the Internet was very useful, but now I've changed my mind."

"Let's hope your new one works better then the one you had before."

@

"Would you like to buy a second-hand computer?"

"I'm afraid not. I'm only able to type with one hand as it is."

Why was the skeleton using the Internet?
To bone up on his schoolwork.

WHY DON'T SKELETONS EXCHANGE E-MAILS?

BECAUSE WE HAVE NO BODY TO DO IT WITH!

Did you hear about the internut who
 spent so long on the web he forgot to
 go to bed?
Eventually it dawned on him.

"Doctor, doctor, I think I'm a computer?"
 "How long have you felt like this?"
 "Ever since I was switched on."

How did the flea learn to use the
 Internet?
He had to start from scratch.

FIRST INTERNUT: Why are you so sad?
SECOND INTERNUT: Last night I sent
 myself an anonymous e-mail and now
 I don't know who it's from.

"Doctor, doctor, I've been spending so
long on the Net that I've started to lose
my memory."
"When did you first notice this?"
"When did I first notice what?"

Why did the internut buy a pair of cowboy
boots?
He wanted to try online dancing.

TEACHER: I've been typing on the Internet
so much, my right hand's begun to
ache.
DOCTOR: That's just age.
TEACHER: But my left hand is just as old
and it doesn't ache at all.

TEACHER: Don't forget to check the Internet if you have trouble with your homework questions.

PUPIL: It's not the questions I have trouble with, it's the answers.

Knock, knock.
Who's there?
Francis.
Francis who?
Francis very easy to contact if you're on the World Wide Web.

"My dog likes to sit down each evening and surf the Net."

"What an intelligent animal!"

"Not really, it took the cat three weeks to teach him."

"Have you seen *www.lockeddoor.com*?"
"Yes, but I found it very difficult to get into."

IF DOORS HAVE A WEBSITE SHOULDN'T WINDOWS HAVE ONE TOO?

WE'D BETTER, OR IT WILL BE CURTAINS FOR US.

Did you hear about the monkey who left bits of his lunch all over the computer?
His dad went bananas.

What did the internut say when someone stole his computer?
e-asy come, e-asy go.

HOW DO BANK ROBBERS SEND MESSAGES?

BY FLEE MAIL!

"Does your mum like shopping on the Internet?"

"No, the trolley keeps rolling off the top of the computer."

"I spent the whole evening knotsurfing"

"Don't you mean netsurfing?"

"No, everyone was complaining because I tied the computer up for ages."

"Doctor, doctor, can I have a bottle of aspirin and a pot of glue?"

"Why?"

"Because I've been at my computer all day and I've got a splitting headache."

"Have you seen the boxing website?"
"Yes, it really knocked me out."

"Can I use your computer to surf the Net?"

"Only if your fingers are less than twelve inches long?"

"Why can't my finger be twelve inches long?"

"Because then it would be a foot"

"I use the Internet to tell me what the weather's like."

"How do you do that?"

"I carry my laptop outside and if it gets wet, I know it's raining."

HAVE YOU SEEN THE UMBRELLA WEBSITE?

YES, BUT IT WENT RIGHT OVER MY HEAD.

How do sheep sign their e-mails?
Ewes sincerely.

"I've been sitting at this computer for hours and I haven't seen a single website."

"That's because you're supposed to sit *facing* the screen."

How do Indian chiefs send messages?
By teepee-mail.

How does Robin Hood send messages around Sherwood Forest?
By tree mail.

INTERNUTTY KNOW-HOW 4

GET CRAFTY!

Surfing the web doesn't mean you have to sit around all day staring at a computer screen. Log on to some of the sites on the opposite page and the last thing you'll have is time on your hands. From games and quizzes you can play with online, to loads of ideas for activities and projects you can get involved with offline, you'll never be bored again (although your P.C. may be . . . with this much stuff to do, it may be quite a while before you get any more free time for surfing!)

CAN I FIND QUIZES ON THE NET?

a) YES
b) NO
c) NONE OF THE ABOVE

http//:www.funology.com

http//:www.kidsdomain.com

http//:www.kiddonet.com

YOU KNOW THERE ISN'T A SINGLE SITE ON THE NET TO HELP YOU MAKE THINGS...

REALLY?

NO-I JUST MADE THAT UP.

GLUE

What do werewolves eat after surfing the Net?
The owner of the Internet cafe.

Who do internuts send their Christmas letters to?
Sant e-claus.

How do you make rude noises on the Internet?
With a whoop e-cushion.

HAVE YOU SEEN THE BAKED BEAN WEBSITE?

I'VE ONLY JUST GOT WIND OF IT.

How do dolphins send messages?
By sea-mail

How do very short people send messages?
By wee-mail.

How do wasps send messages?
By bee-mail.

How do comedians send messages?
By tee-hee mail.

How do English teachers send messages?
By a-e-i-o-u mail.

Why did the gorilla log on to the Internet?
To send chimpanzee-mail.

When do e-mails stop being in black and
   white?
When they are read.

PUPIL: In other schools, pupils get a
   choice of computers to use.
TEACHER: You get a choice here, too.
   Use the one we've got or don't use
   any at all.

Does the school computer have a brother?
No, but it's got lots of tran-sisters.

Why are internuts big headed?
Because they have huge e-gos.

"I've been on my computer all night."
   "Don't you think you'd be more
comfortable on a bed like everyone else?"

What do vampires put at the bottom of
their e-mails?
Best viscious.

@

TEACHER: Look at the state of the school
computer. I want that screen cleaned so
I can see my face in it!
PUPIL: But then it will crack and we won't
be able to use it at all.

"Have you seen
www.smallearthquake.com?"
"Yes, it's no great shakes."

"Have you seen *www.boomerang.com*?"
"Yes, I return to it again and again."

"Have you seen *www.stickytape.com*?"
"Yes, I can't tear myself away."

"I've been e-mailing William
Shakespeare."
   "William Shakespeares's dead, silly."
   "No wonder he hasn't replied."

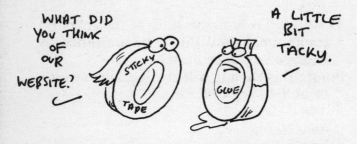

TEACHER: Shall I put the school computer
   on?
PUPIL: No, miss, the dress you're wearing
   looks fine.

"Have you seen *www.yawn.com*?"
"Yes, but I'm a bit tired of it."

"Doctor, doctor, I've been using the Internet a lot and . . ."

"And you think you may need glasses?"

"Why yes, how did you know?"

"It was the way you came in through the window."

WHEN DO COMPUTERS GO TO SLEEP?

WHEN IT'S INTERNIGHT.

P.E. TEACHER: Why did you kick that ball straight at the school computer?

PUPIL: You told me to put it in the Net.

HAVE YOU SEEN WWW.ROTTENTEAM.COM?

YES - I THOUGHT IT WAS MATCHLESS

Who writes hit musicals on the Internet?
Andrew Lloyd Webber.

What do you call an invisible internut?
e-vapourated.

*

What do you get if you cross an elephant
with the Internet?
I don't know, but it's e-nourmous.

I HEAR YOU'VE
BEEN TRACING YOUR
ANCESTORS ON THE
INTERNET...

YES - AND
IT'S A
MAMMOTH
TASK.

Why don't vikings send e-mails?
They prefer to use Norse Code.

What has long ears, hops and likes
websurfing?
The e-aster bunny.

"I've lost my dog."

"Have you tried putting a message on the Internet?"

"Don't be silly, my dog never reads e-mails."

HAVE YOU SEEN THE DALMATION WEBSITE?

NO - HAVEN'T SPOTTED IT SO FAR.

What do you get if you cross the moon with the Internet?
An e-clipse.

"Doctor, doctor, I've been spending so much time on the Net I've started seeing double."

"Really? Please take a seat"

"Which one?"

What do you call a ghost on the Internet?
e-erie.

"I want to explore the Internet, how much do your computers cost?"

"£500 apiece."

"And how much does a whole one cost?"

What do you get if you cross a giant ship with the Internet?

The Site-anic.

Why did the internut try to stretch his
   computer?
Someone told him it had a short circuit.

"Have you seen *www.blottingpaper.com*?"
"Yes, I found it very absorbing."

How do internuts ride horses?
Site-saddle.

HOW DO HORSES SEND MESSAGES?

BY GEEGEE MAIL!

Which Lord Mayor of London was always
   on the Internet?
Click Whittington.

"Doctor, doctor, should I surf the Internet
   on an empty stomach?"
"No, you should do it on a computer."

What do you get if you cross the Internet
with a currant bread?
Spotted Click.

HAVE YOU SEEN THE NEW FRUITCAKE WEBSITE?

YES — IT'S MY CURRANT FAVOURITE!

Who holds up stagecoaches and steals
laptop computers?
Click Turpin.

How do you tell two internuts apart?
e-ny, meany, miney, mo.

"Have you seen *www.tame.com*?"
"Yes, but I'm not wild about it."

HOW DO LIONS RECHARGE THEIR LAPTOPS?

THEY PLUG THEM INTO THE MANES...

What do you call an alien surfing the
    Internet?
e.-t.

"Have you seen *www.square.com*?"
"No, I haven't got around to it."

Who live up in the mountains and are
    always surfing the Net?
The Web-berly Hillbillies.

HAVE YOU HEARD THAT
THERE'S A NEW MOUNTAIN
WEBSITE?

REALLY?
I MUST TAKE
A PEAK AT IT!

What do you get if you cross a flying
    carpet with a computer?
A mouse mat.

What grows on the World Wide Web and
    stings?
Internettles.

*

How do you get rid of internettles?
Always weed your e-mails.

Have you heard about the two internuts
    who got married?
They lived happily webber after.

ANYONE GOT THE
ADDRESS OF THE HORSESHOE
        WEBSITE?

YOU'LL
BE
LUCKY.

What do internuts read instead of books?
Dot comics.

How does Old McDonald send messages?
By e-i-e-i-o-mail.

Who's the biggest Internet fan on the
  magic roundabout?
Webedee.

HOW DO PIGS SURF THE WEB?

ON THE OINKERNET.

Who is the most popular wizard on the
  Internet?
Har e-potter.

INTERNUTTY KNOW-HOW 5

CREATURE FEATURES

If you're an animal lover or concerned about the environment, the Net allows you to bring the whole world of nature into your home or school!

I'VE FOUND A GREAT GARDENING WEBSITE!

I'M GREEN WITH ENVY!

The sites listed below will feed you lots of fascinating facts about the natural world, and also provide information about what you can do to make sure it is around to enjoy when your children's children are internuts, too! (Don't forget to turn the computer off after you've finished surfing – not only is saving energy kinder to the environment, but it'll stop your parents and teachers turning into wild animals!)

ARE YOU AN ENDANGERED SPECIES?

NOT UNTIL MY DAD SEES THE PHONEBILL!

http//:www.nhm.ac.uk

http//:www.bbc.co.uk/nature/

http//.www.kidsplanet.org/

Who sneaked into the three bears' house
  and used their computer?
Gold e-locks.

@

"Doctor, doctor, I keep thinking I'm a
computer."
  "My goodness, you'd better come to my
surgery right away!"
  "I can't, my power cable won't reach
that far."

Who looks after the EuroDisney website?
Mick e-mouse.

Who looks after the chocolate factory
  website?
Will e-wonka.

Why do internuts cry really easily?
They get very e-motional.

What do you call a fire at the Internet cafe?
An e-mergency.

WHO STARTED THE CAMPFIRE WEBSITE?

SOME BRIGHT SPARK

Which of the seven dwarfs use the Internet?
Happ-e, Sleep-e, Grump-e, Dope-e and Sneez-e.

Why doesn't Bashful use the Internet?
e was too shy to tell us.

What about Doc?
e just couldn't be bothered.

How do dustmen surf the web?
On the Bin-ternet.

How do heavy metal bands surf the web?
On the Din-ternet.

How do sharks surf the web?
On the Fin-ternet.

How do barmen surf the web?
On the Gin-ternet.

How do demons surf the web?
On the Sin-ternet.

How does Tom Sawyer surf the web?
On the Huckleberry Finn-ternet.

"Since you've discovered the Internet,
   you don't pay any attention to me!"
"Who said that?"

"Have you seen *www.veryangry.com*?"
   "No, AND STOP ASKING ME STUPID
QUESTIONS!"

What do you call an Internet mystery?
An e-nigma.

How do internuts read each other's minds?
Through e-s.p.

Why did the internut fly though the air?
He was sitting on an e-jector seat.

WHY WAS THE SPRING TIRED?

BECAUSE HE'D STAYED ON THE NET FOR A REALLY LONG STRETCH...

What do you do if the Internet cafe catches fire?
e-vacuate.

What do you get if you cross a computer with a ballet dancer?
The Netcracker Suite.

What goes round the middle of the
 Internet?
The e-quator.

"Have you seen *www.history.com*?"
"Yes, but that was a very long time ago."

How do long distance runners send
 e-mail?
On the Sprin-ternet.

How do pimples send e-mail?
On the Skin-ternet.

How do mountainers send messages?
By ski-mail.

How do footballers send messages?
By referee-mail.

How do children's tv presenters send
   messages?
By dungaree-mail.

How do really posh dogs send messages?
By pedigree-mail.

How do animal lovers send e-mails?
On the Inter-pet.

How do athletes send e-mails?
On the Inter-sweat.

Knock, knock.
Who's there?
Harry.
Harry who?
Harry up and finish netsurfing,
I want a go.

Knock, knock.
Who's there?
Luke.
Luke who?
Luke at your e-mails, I'm tired of waiting.

"Have you seen *www.busfull.com*?"
"No, I'm afraid that one passed me by."

HAVE YOU SEEN
THE BUS WEBSITE?

YES — IT'S
JUST
THE TICKET.

STOP

Why are frogs no good at websurfing?
Computers have them toad-ily confused.

"Have you seen *www.pitchdark.com*?"
"Yes, but I really couldn't see what all the
fuss is about."

"Why did the vampire stop netsurfing at 11 o'clock?"
"It was time for his coffin break."

What do Internuts get when they eat too fast?
The Clickups.

What do internuts have in their knickers?
e-lastic.

"Have you seen *www.laryngitis.com*?"
"Can't say I have."

INTERNUTTY KNOW-HOW 6

HOME SWEET HOMEWORK

Not many people enjoy doing homework, whether it's on a computer or plain old pen and paper. But at least the Internet allows you to find that missing date or fiddly fact that would otherwise drive you bonkers.

The sites listed below should help you find most pieces of information that you need, but try to use the facts as a starter for your own writing rather than simply copying straight from the screen. If you practise using your own brain a little, you'll soon find that the most powerful computer of all is right inside your head.

http//:www.letsfindout.com

http//:www.homeworkelephant.co.uk

http//:www.bbc.co.uk/education

How do you find white shirts on the
  Internet?
Use a starch engine.

Have you heard abut the two internuts
  who got married?
They were newlywebs.

Which football team do you need to
  connect up your computer?
Leeds.

"Do you like the new trousers website?"
"No, it's pants."

How does Christopher Robin websurf?
On his com-pooh-ter.

"Have you seen *www.brokenglass.com*?"
"Yes, but it's not all it's cracked up to be."

@

Knock, knock.
Who's there?
Howie.
Howie who?
Howie Nearth can you answer e-mails when you have your nose in this stupid joke book all day?

YOU NEED TO LOG ON TO THE WINDOW REPAIR WEBSITE!

I DID — BUT IT GAVE ME A PANE!

"Have you seen *www.stewedprunes.com*?"
"Yes, it really got me going."

*

Why do internuts write joke books?
For their own e-musement.

Why is this the last internut joke?
Because everyone's had e-nough.

ALL'S WEB THAT ENDS WEB...
HOPE TO "E" YOU ALL
AGAIN SOON!

LITTLE BOOKS OF COOL!

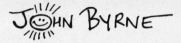

Packed with top tips, great gags and crazy cartoons, these little books will help you breeze through life without ever losing your cool!

The Little Book of Cool at School

If you're having trouble with teachers or finding maths monstrous this little book will make a big difference to how you feel and help you stay calm in the classroom.

ISBN 0 09 940336 6 £1.99

The Little Book of Summer Cool

This book has all you need to make sure that rain or shine your summer hols are fun, fun, fun!

ISBN 0 09 941116 4 £1.99

The Little Book of Cool at Christmas

Christmas can be very stressful with family feuds and pricey presents but with this little book you can make sure yuletime is a cool time.

ISBN 0 09 940791 4 £1.99

THE BULLYBUSTERS

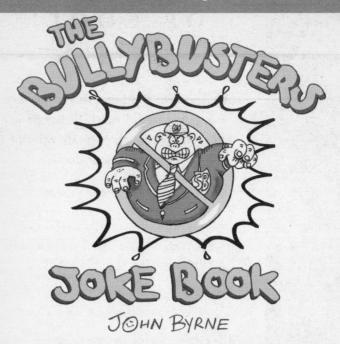

JOKE BOOK

JOHN BYRNE

Bullies *are* losers, big time! But lets face it,
telling them you think that can be a bit tricky.
So what's the solution?

GET BULLYBUSTING!

Here are hundreds of brilliant bully put-downs,
jokes and back-answers to give you a
seriously funny start. So next
time a bully bothers you, you
can make sure the joke
will be on them.

WITTY WAYS TO
KNOCK BULLIES
FOR SIX!